Original title:
Beyond Bad Habits

Copyright © 2024 Creative Arts Management OÜ
All rights reserved.

Author: Tim Wood
ISBN HARDBACK: 978-9916-88-426-3
ISBN PAPERBACK: 978-9916-88-427-0

Healing through New Horizons

In the dawn's soft light, we rise anew,
Casting aside shadows that once grew.
With every step, hope's whisper sings,
Embracing the warmth that new life brings.

Mountains stand tall, yet we climb higher,
Facing our fears, igniting the fire.
With every breath, we find our way,
Towards brighter skies, a brand new day.

The heart mends slow, like a budding flower,
Each petal unfolds, reclaiming power.
Through storms we weather, we learn to sway,
Finding ourselves in the light of day.

Horizons expand, inviting the vast,
Leaving behind the pain of the past.
In every ending, a new start blooms,
Together we rise, dispelling the glooms.

Crafting a Life of Intent

With each choice, we sketch our way,
Every moment, a brush to play.
We build our dreams with steady hands,
In the silence, our heart understands.

Intentions whispered in the night,
Guiding us under soft moonlight.
A canvas bright, a tale to weave,
In the art of living, we believe.

The Formula of Fresh Starts

Counting blessings, letting go,
In the cycle, we find flow.
Pages turning, a brand new year,
With courage, we conquer fear.

New horizons call our name,
Embracing shadows without blame.
In each sunrise, possibilities grow,
With fresh beginnings, our spirits glow.

Sailing into New Waters

Set the sails and catch the breeze,
Adventure waits beyond the trees.
Every wave a chance to learn,
In the currents, our hearts yearn.

Navigating with stars above,
Finding solace, sharing love.
In uncharted depths, we chart our course,
Every journey fueled by force.

The Dawn of Awareness

As daylight breaks, we start to see,
The gentle dance of possibility.
In stillness found, we hold the key,
Awakening to what can be.

Moments linger, the heart can feel,
Connecting dots to what is real.
With open eyes, we walk the path,
In the dawn, we find our math.

Igniting the Fire of Intent

Within the heart, a spark ignites,
Dreams take wing, soaring heights.
Purpose shines, a guiding light,
Focus sharpens in the night.

With each step, the path unfolds,
Courage grows, as dreams are told.
Intent weaves through the mundane,
Transforming loss into gain.

Blossoming into Wholeness

Petals open to greet the sun,
Each breath a dance, life well begun.
Colors merge, a vibrant hue,
Embracing all, the old and new.

Roots grow deep in nourishing soil,
Tending fears, through love we toil.
In stillness, we find our grace,
A journey shared, a sacred space.

The Power of Resilience

Through storms we bend, yet do not break,
In every trial, a lesson takes.
Stand tall like trees in the fierce wind,
With every challenge, strength begins.

Mountains loom, but we will climb,
One step forward, we take our time.
Hope ignites in darkest night,
A beacon shining, pure and bright.

Listening to the Call of Change

Whispers echo in the still air,
A gentle nudge, urging to care.
Seasons shift, as we must grow,
Embrace the tide and let it flow.

Change unfolds like a soft breeze,
Inviting us to bend our knees.
In each farewell, a greeting near,
For new beginnings, I hold dear.

Dancing with Discontent

In shadows deep where whispers sigh,
We twirl around the dreams gone by.
A silent scream, a masked embrace,
In discontent, we find our place.

The music plays, a haunting tune,
Under the light of a pale moon.
With every step, we choose to fight,
In the dark, we seek the light.

The Alchemy of Reflection

Mirrors catch the glint of time,
In stillness, truths begin to chime.
Transformation takes its gentle hold,
In quiet moments, stories unfold.

Shadows blend with colors bright,
Casting doubt into the night.
From ashes rise the dreams anew,
In reflection, we find the view.

Resilience in the Night

Stars flicker in the velvet dark,
Each one holds a tiny spark.
Through trials faced and battles won,
Resilience shines just like the sun.

With every tear, a lesson learned,
In the night, our spirits burned.
We rise again, unbowed, unbent,
In the silence, strength is meant.

Seeds of a New Dawn

Beneath the soil, a promise lies,
In hidden depths, hope gently sighs.
With patience, light begins to breach,
The dreams we sow, the love we teach.

The sky awakens with colors bright,
Each morning brings a fresh delight.
As petals bloom in warm embrace,
The seeds of dawn, we now must trace.

The Symphony of Inner Strength

In quiet moments, courage grows,
A whisper soft beneath the blows.
Each heartbeat sings a powerful tune,
Resilience rising with the moon.

Through shadows cast, the light will gleam,
With fractured dreams, we forge the theme.
A symphony of grit and grace,
In every trial, we find our place.

The storms may howl, our spirits high,
We'll dance on winds, learn how to fly.
With every note, our spirits blend,
In harmony, we will ascend.

Cultivating the Habit of Hope

In the garden of our mind,
Seeds of dreams, we'll gently find.
Watered with love, sunshine bright,
Hope will bloom, a vivid sight.

With every breath, we sow our fate,
Nurtured by both love and weight.
In darkest soil, the bright can rise,
Reaching ever for the skies.

With patience strong and arms out wide,
Together facing any tide.
We'll build a world where hearts can cope,
In every corner, spread our hope.

From Ashes to Aspiration

From ashes cold, a spark ignites,
In darkest nights, we find our sights.
Like phoenix proud, we take to flight,
Reborn anew in morning light.

Each lesson learned from loss and pain,
A testament that we can gain.
With every challenge, strength we know,
From humble earth, our spirits grow.

We'll write a tale of dreams embraced,
With wisdom earned, our fears displaced.
In every heart, a fire will blaze,
From ashes wise, we rise always.

In Search of Brighter Days

In the whispers of the dawn,
We search for light, to carry on.
With every step, hope winds its way,
Through cloudy paths towards the bay.

With opened hearts, we seek the sun,
In every moment, we become.
A gentle breeze, the warmth of grace,
In every trial, we find our place.

With stories shared and hands held tight,
Together facing every night.
For in this quest, our dreams will sway,
In search of love, we'll find our way.

The Flourish of Intent

In gardens where the dreams take flight,
Intentions bloom in morning light.
Nurtured well with hopes and care,
Life unfolds, as we lay bare.

Each seed we plant, each thought we weave,
Shapes the world that we believe.
In every action, truth resides,
A flourish found where love abides.

Navigating Through Change

Waves of change crash on the shore,
Whispers beckon, urge for more.
With every tide, the past drifts away,
New horizons beckon, lead the way.

Embrace the unknown, let it flow,
In shifting sands, new paths will grow.
With courage found in heart's refrain,
We find our strength, despite the strain.

The Gift of Second Chances

Every dawn, a chance to start,
With open arms and willing heart.
Mistakes once made are lessons learned,
In every fall, new courage burned.

Forgive the past, let shadows fade,
In second acts, hope will cascade.
Life's beautiful dance, a tender prance,
Opportunity calls, take the chance.

Beyond the Mirror of Reflection

In the glass, truths may collide,
A deeper gaze reveals inside.
Facets of self, both bright and dim,
In every flaw, our spirits swim.

Beyond the surface, beauty lies,
In every tear, in every rise.
Embrace the journey, shape our fate,
In the mirror's truth, we create.

A Tapestry of Forgiveness

In shadows deep, we weave our threads,
With colors bright, where kindness spreads.
Each stitch a tale, of pain and grace,
In the heart's loom, we find our place.

Let go the chains that bind the soul,
In open hands, we find the whole.
A tapestry rich, in hues of light,
Forgiveness glows, dispelling night.

Rebirth in the Moment

Each breath a chance, a brand new start,
In fleeting time, we play our part.
With every dawn, our spirit grows,
In the silence, the stillness flows.

Awake in joy, the world anew,
The past behind, the future true.
Rebirth unfolds, like flowers bloom,
Embrace the now, dispel the gloom.

Charting My Own Course

Upon the waves, my ship will sail,
With compass set, I shall not fail.
The winds of fate may shift and change,
But in my heart, I'll rearrange.

With courage strong, I'll steer the way,
Guided by stars, I'll not dismay.
Each wave I ride, a story told,
In every challenge, I find bold.

The Reflection of Growth

In mirrors clear, the past does reflect,
With every scar, a deep respect.
Seeds of wisdom from trials sown,
In every loss, I've truly grown.

Roots run deep, through storm and sun,
In life's vast garden, I am one.
Blooming brightly, in colors bold,
The reflection speaks, my spirit's gold.

The Victory of Will

In a world of doubt, we stand tall,
Our hearts are fierce, we won't fall.
With every challenge that we face,
We rise with strength, we find our place.

Through storms of fear, we push ahead,
With dreams alive, and hope widespread.
The fire within ignites our soul,
In unity, we feel the whole.

No chains can bind what we have sought,
With passion driven, battles fought.
Our spirits soar, we won't retreat,
The victory of will, so sweet.

Together we create our fate,
In action bold, we celebrate.
The path is hard, yet still we climb,
A testament to strength and time.

A Dance with Discipline

Step by step, we find our grace,
In every challenge, a new embrace.
With rhythm strong, we move as one,
In this dance, we shine like the sun.

Through the trials, we learn to flow,
With consistency, our spirits grow.
Each decision, a beat in time,
In the dance of life, we find our rhyme.

The art of balance, a mindful sway,
In discipline, we carve our way.
Strength in repetition, it brings us near,
In every motion, we conquer fear.

Together we leap, we twirl, we spin,
In the heart's rhythm, we all win.
A dance with discipline, bold and free,
In every step, we find harmony.

Breaking Chains of Routine

In the monotony, we seek a spark,
Breaking free, we make our mark.
With open minds, we shed the past,
Creating paths that ever last.

No longer bound by the daily grind,
In every step, new worlds we find.
With courage deep, we start anew,
Each moment fresh, each day a cue.

In the stillness, we hear a song,
A melody where we belong.
With every choice, we shift the fate,
Breaking chains, we celebrate.

Together we rise, ignite the flame,
In this journey, we play the game.
No more routine, just dreams to chase,
Stepping forward into open space.

Shadows of Old Patterns

In shadows cast by memories steep,
We tread softly, our journey deep.
The echoes of choices, they haunt our way,
Yet in their whispers, we find our sway.

With every step, we break the mold,
In courage found, our hearts unfold.
Letting go of what's held too tight,
We seek the dawn, we seek the light.

Through struggles faced and battles fought,
In the tapestry, lessons are wrought.
The shadows fade with every breath,
In the light of change, we conquer death.

Together we rise, unchained and bold,
In the arms of freedom, our lives unfold.
Shadows of old, we leave behind,
In the embrace of hope, we find our kind.

The Bridge to a Clearer Mind

Across the waters, calm and wide,
Thoughts can flow, no need to hide.
With each step, clarity grows,
A gentle path, where wisdom flows.

Whispers of peace dance on the breeze,
Releasing burdens, heart finds ease.
A bridge that leads to thoughts refined,
Embracing all, a clearer mind.

Painting Life with New Colors

With every brush, a story's told,
A splash of red, a touch of gold.
Life's canvas waits, both bright and vast,
Moments shared, the die is cast.

Blues of sorrow, greens of joy,
Each stroke, a memory to deploy.
Painting dreams with vibrant hue,
Transforming grey to vibrant blue.

Mending Broken Patterns

Threads of time begin to fray,
Patterns lost along the way.
Stitches firm, with care and grace,
Hearts and minds find their place.

In each tear, a chance to heal,
Resilience born from the ordeal.
Mending what once seemed apart,
A tapestry of hope, a brand new start.

From Chains to Stargazing

In shadows cast by heavy chains,
Hope flickers softly, yet remains.
Each link whispers of dreams confined,
Yet starlit skies invite the mind.

Breaking free, the night unfolds,
With open hearts, a future bold.
From darkness deep, the journey takes,
To starlit dreams, where freedom wakes.

Embracing Change Like a Friend

In whispers soft, the winds do call,
Embrace each twist, let worries fall.
With open arms, we greet the dawn,
In every new path, new hope is drawn.

Transformation sings a gentle tune,
Each step we take, beneath the moon.
Like seasons shift, we too must sway,
Find strength in change, come what may.

Chasing Sunsets of Renewal

The sky ablaze, a fiery hue,
In every sunset, dreams renew.
We chase the light that bids goodbye,
In twilight's glow, our spirits fly.

With every dusk, a promise made,
Tomorrow's light will never fade.
So let the colors blend and dance,
In the twilight's embrace, we take our chance.

The Mosaic of Daily Choices

Each choice a tile, in life's great wall,
A vibrant pattern, both large and small.
In mundane moments, magic unfolds,
A tapestry woven with stories told.

With every dawn, new hues collide,
In paths we take, let love be our guide.
We craft our fate with every glance,
In this mosaic, find your dance.

Emerging from the Shadows

From shadows deep, we seek the light,
In courage found, we rise from night.
With every step, a story begins,
Through whispered doubts, our strength wins.

The dawn breaks forth, a tender embrace,
In healing rays, we find our place.
From ashes born, like phoenix yore,
We rise anew, forevermore.

Whispers of a New Start

In the dawn's gentle light,
Hope dances on the breeze,
Whispers of a new day,
Easing the heart's unease.

Footsteps on a soft path,
Each moment feels so clear,
Dreams awaken within,
Erasing every fear.

With each breath that we take,
The past starts to release,
New beginnings bloom fresh,
In a garden of peace.

Breaking the Silence of Routine

Shattered glass of the ordinary,
A spark ignites the night,
Routine fades in the shadows,
As dreams take to flight.

The clock ticks softly by,
Yet time begins to bend,
Moments stretch and expand,
To where new paths ascend.

With courage as our guide,
We leap into the unknown,
Breaking chains of the past,
Finding a place called home.

A Celebration of Fresh Paths

New trails lie before us,
With sunlit ways to roam,
Every step a celebration,
As we carve out our home.

Laughter fills the air,
With friends who walk beside,
Embracing the unknown,
With hearts open wide.

Challenges may arise,
Yet joy fuels our pace,
Together we will wander,
In this beautiful space.

The Constellation of New Dreams

Stars twinkle with promise,
A canvas of the night,
Dreams shimmer like constellations,
Guiding us to the light.

Every wish takes its form,
As we reach for the sky,
Painting our aspirations,
With colors that amplify.

In the quiet of hope,
New adventures take flight,
Together we will follow,
The path that feels right.

Dancing with New Beginnings

In the dawn of light, we sway,
New dreams begin to play,
With every turn, hope ignites,
A dance of joy, through days and nights.

Step by step, the rhythms flow,
Embracing change, we learn to grow,
Every twirl, a fresh start found,
In our hearts, love's melody sounds.

With open arms, we greet the dawn,
As shadows fade, new paths are drawn,
In every leap, the past we shed,
To the beat of life, we're gently led.

Together we move, hand in hand,
In this journey, we'll make our stand,
With laughter bright and spirits free,
In dancing light, we live to be.

A Pathway to Renewal

Through winding roads, we take our stand,
Each step a chance, a guiding hand,
Leaves of change fall soft around,
In stillness, solutions are found.

Waves of doubt may crash and rise,
Yet through the storms, we see the skies,
The heart's echo calls us near,
With every whisper, we conquer fear.

Moments linger, lessons learned,
In quiet growth, the spirit yearns,
The path unfolds, a tapestry,
Woven threads of destiny.

In the garden of our mind,
Roots of hope and strength entwined,
We'll nurture dreams that spring anew,
To find the light and nurture truth.

Tides of Transformation

Like waves that crash upon the shore,
Change dances lightly, asks for more,
With each retreat, a lesson stays,
In ebb and flow of life's great ways.

With open hearts, we let it be,
As currents shift, we learn to see,
The tides of fate, both wild and free,
Guide our souls to who we're meant to be.

Merging waters, past and now,
In the moment, we take a bow,
From deep within, the changes rise,
A rebirth seen through hopeful eyes.

Together we'll sail, brave the quest,
In transformation, we are blessed,
For every challenge meets its end,
In life's embrace, we find our mend.

Rewriting the Scripts of Tomorrow

With pens in hand, we build anew,
Stories waiting for me and you,
Each word a spark, igniting fire,
To fill our hearts with pure desire.

In every chapter, dreams repose,
Transforming pain into a rose,
The ink flows freely, fresh and bright,
Guiding shadows into light.

Our hands create the tales we tell,
Of journeys lived, through joy and hell,
With courage strong, we turn the page,
Embracing life at every stage.

So let us write without regret,
In every word, our goals are set,
For tomorrow waits, let's set it free,
In storytelling, we find our key.

Heartbeats of a New Dawn

Whispers of the morning light,
Awakening the world in grace.
Each heartbeat sings a sweet delight,
A fresh beginning we embrace.

Fingers trace the dewy air,
Hope dances on the breeze.
In every moment, love laid bare,
Life unfolds with gentle ease.

The sky blushes as stars retreat,
Colors burst like laughter's sound.
With every step, the rhythm's beat,
New dreams awaken, unbound.

Together we shall journey forth,
With hearts aglow, we chase the day.
In unity, we find our worth,
Heartbeats lead us on our way.

Unraveling the Comfort Zone

Nestled warm in thoughts we cling,
Familiar paths we often tread.
Yet whispers call; our hearts take wing,
Awakening the dreams we've fed.

Stepping out, the ground feels strange,
New horizons beckon wide.
With every choice, we find the change,
A brighter world; our fears subside.

The comfort fades, but courage grows,
In shadows cast, we find the light.
Journeying forth where wild wind blows,
Adventure sparks within our sight.

So take my hand, let's explore,
With open hearts, we'll seize the day.
In every risk, there's so much more,
Unraveling, we find our way.

Surrendering to Growth

In silence lies the chance to bloom,
Roots entwined with strength and grace.
As seasons shift, we shed the gloom,
Embracing life at our own pace.

Let go the fears that weigh us down,
Like leaves drifting in the fall.
With open hearts, we'll wear our crown,
For in surrender, we stand tall.

Each challenge faced, a lesson learned,
A fire ignites within our soul.
Through trials, wisdom has returned,
In every struggle, we feel whole.

With every heartbeat, we transform,
Nature's call guides us to heal.
Surrender fills our hearts with warmth,
Growth unveils what's truly real.

Dreaming in Stride

With open eyes, we chase the stars,
Each dream a compass, guiding light.
Across the fields, we bear no scars,
In every step, we dare to fight.

Voices whisper of paths unknown,
Together, we'll forge ahead.
With hopes ignited, seeds are sown,
In every stride, the future's bred.

Through valleys deep and mountains high,
Our spirits soar on wings of trust.
We paint the canvas of the sky,
And turn our dreams to vibrant dust.

So let us dance with fate's embrace,
Fearing not what lies in store.
With hearts afire, we'll find our place,
Dreaming onward, evermore.

Chasing the Fractured Self

In mirrors cracked, I seek my face,
Shadows dance in a tight embrace.
Fragments whisper tales of old,
Through hidden paths, my truth unfolds.

Whispers echo in the night,
Each step forward, a gentle fight.
Lost pieces call from deep within,
A puzzle where my soul can spin.

Through fractured dreams and fleeting sights,
I chase the dawn, escape the nights.
The road ahead is winding still,
Yet, with each breath, I find my will.

In every scar, a story waits,
A testament to broken fates.
Embracing all, I stand and rise,
A whole once more, beneath the skies.

Silencing the Siren's Call

In waves of whispers, she does hum,
A haunting voice that makes me numb.
Yet in the depths, I find my fight,
To cut the ties and seek the light.

With every surge, the fears parade,
A siren's song, a sweet charade.
Yet wisdom grows where silence reigns,
And in the quiet, peace remains.

I cast my net to still the waves,
Invest in strength, the soul it saves.
The call may fade, but I stand tall,
A sentinel against her thrall.

Through tranquil shores, I walk anew,
No longer lost, a clearer view.
With courage found, I break the spell,
In silence, hear my heart's own swell.

Mapping the Inner Landscape

With compass drawn, I take a stand,
To map the realms of my own land.
Each thought a mountain, each fear a sea,
In every valley, a part of me.

Paths entwine like branches wide,
A forest deep where secrets hide.
In shadows cast, my courage blooms,
As sunlight breaks through ancient tombs.

Every scar a marked terrain,
A journey rich with joy and pain.
With ink and brush, I sketch and strive,
To bring each raw emotion alive.

An atlas made of breath and flesh,
In every corner, dreams enmesh.
To know the map is to be whole,
An exploration of the soul.

A Symphony of Self-Discovery

In chords of silence, notes arise,
Each heartbeat sings, a sweet surprise.
Through valleys low and mountains high,
A melody where spirits fly.

The whispers of the past do blend,
In harmonies that twist and bend.
Each note, a layer of my core,
Resonates with truth and more.

As rhythms shift, I dance and sway,
Unraveling fears along the way.
In every stir, a spark of grace,
A symphony I can embrace.

With every sound, my essence grows,
A tapestry of highs and lows.
In this concerto, I take my part,
A symphony that plays my heart.

Threads of Reinvention

In shadows cast by doubt anew,
We weave our dreams from threads so true.
With every stitch, a story grows,
A tapestry of hope that glows.

Through trials faced, we rise and mend,
Embracing change, we start to blend.
The colors bright, the patterns bold,
In every heart, a tale unfolds.

As seasons shift and time moves past,
We find our strength, we learn at last.
With each renewal comes a chance,
To sway with life's enchanting dance.

Beneath the stars, our spirits soar,
A journey shared forevermore.
With threads of love, we intertwine,
And craft a world where we all shine.

A Canvas of Better Choices

A canvas waits, so blank and wide,
With brushes armed, we will decide.
The colors bright, the tones defined,
Each stroke a choice, a thought combined.

In every hue, a lesson learned,
In every twist, the heart discerned.
With patience, we can start to see,
The artwork grows, we set it free.

The shadows blend with vibrant light,
In darkest hours, we seek the bright.
Each choice we make, a pathway drawn,
To chase the dusk and greet the dawn.

A masterpiece, we craft each day,
With hopes and dreams, we find our way.
In every choice, we shape our fate,
On this canvas, we celebrate.

The Journey of the Reformed

With steps unsteady, yet so bold,
A heart, once heavy, now unfolds.
Each moment brings a chance renewed,
In every breath, we find our mood.

The road is long, with twists and turns,
In every lesson, deep love burns.
With every scar, we gain our grace,
The journey taught, we now embrace.

The past, a whisper, fades away,
We choose the light, we seize the day.
With hands uplifted, spirits high,
In unity, we learn to fly.

Together here, we tread as one,
A story forged, our work begun.
The journey rich, with joy adorned,
In every heart, the reformed.

Finding Beauty in Discipline

In quiet hours, we shape our way,
Through rhythmic acts, we learn and play.
The beauty found in ordered tasks,
As purpose grows, the soul unmasked.

With steady hands, we craft and mold,
Through trials faced, our spirits bold.
In every habit, strength revealed,
A garden sown, our hearts unsealed.

The daily grind, a sacred rite,
Transforming darkness into light.
Through discipline, we reawaken,
The dreams and goals that cannot be shaken.

In every moment, grace aligned,
A symphony of heart and mind.
Finding beauty as we strive,
In the dance of life, we thrive.

The Alchemy of Change

In shadows thick, a spark ignites,
Transforming fear into new sights.
The past a whisper, the future bright,
With every step, we embrace the light.

A tapestry woven with threads of fate,
In each mistake, we cultivate.
The phoenix rises from ash and glow,
With heart wide open, we learn to grow.

Beneath the storms, a calm will rise,
In every ending, a new surprise.
We shed old skin, emerge anew,
The alchemy of change is calling you.

Wings of Fresh Intentions

With every dawn, the promise flows,
A breeze that carries hope and grows.
Wings outstretched toward the skies,
In pure ambition, our spirit flies.

Each whispered wish, a gentle guide,
In every heart, dreams coincide.
With courage fierce and visions clear,
We lift our wings, we have no fear.

The path unfolds, a canvas wide,
With fresh intentions, we abide.
In unity, we find our way,
With wings of light, we greet the day.

Echoes of Resilience

In depths of silence, strength takes form,
Through crack and crevice, we weather the storm.
With voices strong, we rise and dare,
Echoes of resilience fill the air.

In moments bleak, when hope seems far,
We look within, our guiding star.
Through trials faced and burdens borne,
Emerging bright, we are reborn.

We weave our stories, thread by thread,
In every challenge, we forge ahead.
With hearts unyielding, we stand as one,
In echoes of resilience, we've just begun.

The Art of Letting Go

In gentle whispers, we learn to release,
To find within our hearts, a peace.
With every breath, we shed the weight,
The art of letting go, our fate.

Like autumn leaves that dance and sway,
We learn to trust, to guide our way.
In every ending, a door to new,
With grace and love, we start anew.

We hold the memories, but not the pain,
For in the loss, there's much to gain.
With open hands, we find our flow,
This is the essence of letting go.

Breaking the Mirror

In shattered glass, reflections fade,
A glimpse of truth, so softly laid.
Echoes whisper, secrets in night,
In the fractures, find your light.

The image shifts, a dance with doubt,
What's inside, we often scout.
Yet from the pieces, strength shall rise,
A brave new self, beyond disguise.

Each shard a story, a tale retold,
Of battles fought and dreams of gold.
Through jagged edges, we pave a way,
To face the dawn of a brand new day.

So gaze again, but see with grace,
The beauty lies in every trace.
Embrace the cracks, let the light pour in,
For in breaking, we learn to begin.

Compass of the Heart

In the silence, a whisper calls,
A gentle pull as daylight falls.
Wanderers seek, both near and far,
Guided by love, their shining star.

Through winding paths and branches wide,
A map unfolds, with hope as guide.
With every beat, the compass spins,
Charting where the journey begins.

Mountains high and valleys low,
The heart knows truth we often forego.
In every turn, a lesson learned,
The fire within forever burned.

So follow the signs that lead you true,
Listen closely to what feels new.
For in the heart, the compass lies,
A beacon bright beneath the skies.

Anchors to the Soul

In tempest tides, we drift and sway,
Yet find our ground in softest clay.
With roots that dig, so deep, so true,
   Empowered by the love we grew.

Through storms that rage and nights so long,
   We hold on tight, our spirits strong.
The anchor lies in hearts entwined,
   A bond unbreakable, forever bind.

In quiet moments, still we stand,
Together, side by side, hand in hand.
Though waves may crash and winds may howl,
   We navigate life's unknown prowl.

Our anchors steady in every storm,
   Creating space for love to warm.
In every challenge, we won't let go,
For in each other's strength, we grow.

Beyond the Comfort Zone

In whispers soft, the comfort sings,
Yet outside lies what daring brings.
With every step into the unknown,
We carve new paths, the seeds are sown.

Fear may linger, shadows may play,
But courage calls, a bright new day.
With hearts aflame, we take the leap,
To push the limits, no time for sleep.

In the wild, we shed our fears,
With open hearts and joyful tears.
The world expands, horizons gleam,
Beyond the zone, we chase the dream.

So step outside, embrace the thrill,
For in the risk, we learn our will.
Beyond the comfort, life awaits,
A vibrant canvas, destiny creates.

The Voyage of Self-Discovery

Across the sea of thoughts, I sail,
Charting the course where dreams prevail.
Waves of doubt crash on the shore,
Yet within me lies an open door.

With each gust of wind, I learn to steer,
Facing my fears, I persevere.
Stars above guide my wandering heart,
In the depths of me, I find a spark.

Islands of hope beckon with light,
Through stormy nights, I embrace the fight.
Mapping the silence of my own soul,
With every step, I begin to feel whole.

The voyage continues, a sacred quest,
In the stillness, I finally rest.
The compass within, a guiding flame,
In this journey, I forge my name.

Healing the Wounds of Yesterday

In the shadows of pain, I tread light,
Each scar a story, a silent fight.
I gather the pieces, thread by thread,
In the embrace of time, I find the dead.

Wounds may linger, but I shall mend,
With grace as my guide and love to lend.
The past is a canvas, colors to blend,
With each stroke, a message to send.

I breathe in the lessons, exhale the tears,
Transforming my sorrow, confronting my fears.
Each moment a step, I choose to grow,
In the garden of healing, I plant and sow.

Tomorrow awaits with a gentle call,
A tapestry woven, I won't let it fall.
With every sunrise, I rise anew,
In the strength of my heart, I find the true.

The Change I've Yearned For

In the depths of my heart, I long for change,
To break from the bonds, to rearrange.
Shadows of fear loom over my way,
Yet within me whispers the promise of day.

I gather my courage, a spark in the dark,
Taking the leap, igniting the spark.
Every step forward, a glimmer of light,
In the dance of the moments, I grasp what is right.

The chains of the past begin to fade,
With every intention, the path is laid.
I surrender to growth, a river so wild,
Embracing my journey, forever a child.

The chorus of change sings deep in my soul,
A symphony rising, making me whole.
In the arms of the future, I spin and twirl,
With hope as my anchor, I embrace the whirl.

Learning to Dance with Discomfort

In the quiet chaos, I find my place,
Discomfort whispers with a gentle grace.
I sway in the tension, a rhythm to glean,
In the echoes of struggle, I learn to be seen.

Step by step, I move through the ache,
Finding the joy that discomfort can make.
The laughter of challenge, a playful refrain,
In the dance of my heart, I embrace the pain.

With each twist and turn, I gain my power,
Turning the moments into flowers.
The struggle is real, but so is the bliss,
In the risky embrace, I find my true kiss.

So I dance through the fire, I spin through the storm,
In learning to sway, I break from the norm.
Discomfort my partner, we twirl and we sway,
In the dance of my life, I find my own way.

Threads of Resistance

In shadows deep, we weave our dreams,
A tapestry of silent screams.
With every stitch, we stand our ground,
In whispered strength, our voices sound.

The fabric worn, yet strong and bold,
A history in fibers told.
Together we rise, we break the chain,
From every loss, we learn from pain.

In the dark, resilience grows,
A vibrant path, where courage flows.
Through every struggle, hearts ignite,
Our threads of hope, a guiding light.

Against the odds, we carve our way,
In unity, we find our sway.
Each strand a story, each knot a bond,
In threads of resistance, we respond.

Echoes of Transformation

In tranquil pools, the ripples dance,
Life's shifting form, a fleeting chance.
With every wave, we change our face,
In every echo, we find our place.

The past may call, but we move on,
Embracing light as shadows yawn.
With open hearts, we learn to grow,
Through every trial, new seeds we sow.

The whispers soft, they guide the way,
From dusk to dawn, into the fray.
With courage fierce and spirits high,
We break the dawn, and touch the sky.

In transformation's tender embrace,
We find our strength, we find our grace.
From echoes past, a new song sings,
In every moment, our future springs.

Unmasking the Familiar

Beneath the veil of daily lives,
The unseen truth quietly strives.
In patterns worn, we often hide,
Unmasking worlds where dreams reside.

The ordinary blooms anew,
In hidden realms, we shape what's true.
With every glance, the layers peel,
What once was lost, we learn to feel.

In mirrored walls, reflections change,
Familiar faces, now rearranged.
Behind each smile, a story waits,
In whispered tales, destiny narrates.

Step boldly forth, embrace the night,
In shadows cast, there shines a light.
To unmask life is to be free,
In every heart, the key is she.

In the Light of Change

Dawn breaks gently, painting skies,
A canvas bright where hope will rise.
With every breath, a chance to see,
In the light of change, we find our glee.

The winds of fate, they shift and sway,
But steadfast hearts won't turn away.
For in the winds, there lies a spark,
A guiding flame against the dark.

With courage drawn from deep within,
We face the storms, and thus begin.
In every trial, we learn to bend,
For change, dear friend, is not the end.

So let us dance in morning's glow,
Embrace the light, let courage flow.
Together we rise, unbound, we soar,
In the light of change, we live for more.

Breaking the Chains of Routine

In the dawn's gentle light, we rise,
Breaking free from the past's tight ties.
Each moment a chance, a spark of change,
Embrace the unknown, let life rearrange.

Step by step, we dance with grace,
In pursuits new, we find our place.
No longer bound, we stretch our hands,
To forge our dreams on shifting sands.

With courage held close, we face each day,
Transforming the mundane, come what may.
The chains that once held us now fall away,
In the rhythm of life, we choose to sway.

So lift your heart, let joy take flight,
In this bold journey, we find our light.
Together we'll shatter the walls of despair,
And write our own stories, the world we'll share.

Shadows of Temptation

Whispers in twilight, calling my name,
Shadows that flicker, igniting the flame.
Desires that linger, so sweetly they glide,
In the depths of my heart, they cleverly hide.

Moments of weakness, the pull of the night,
Chasing the echo, the thrill and the fright.
Every choice weighs heavy, a dance on the edge,
Will I break the silence or step from the ledge?

Yet still in the darkness, a voice breaks the chains,
It sings of redemption, of love's gentle reins.
Through the fog of confusion, I seek to align,
Choosing the path where the sun will still shine.

In shadows I wander, but I long for the light,
To banish temptation, embrace what feels right.
With courage I step, through the whispers that call,
For in understanding, I shall rise or fall.

Whispers of Renewal

Through cracks in the earth, life starts to bloom,
A promise of growth, dispelling the gloom.
With each tender breeze, sweet whispers arise,
Calling forth strength from the depths of the skies.

Hope dances lightly on petals anew,
Painting the world in fresh shades and hues.
Every heartbeat echoes with life's refrain,
In the silent moments, shed loss and gain.

Look to the dawn, let it guide our way,
With wisdom that shimmers as night turns to day.
This cycle of change, a wondrous embrace,
Each ending a start, in time's endless space.

So let us awaken, let dreams take their flight,
With whispers that beckon through shadows of night.
In the tapestry woven by heartbeats and tears,
We'll find our renewal, conquering fears.

The Path to Unraveled Patterns

In the maze of habit, we tread with care,
Tracing lines familiar, a quiet despair.
Yet somewhere within, a spark dares to glow,
Inviting the wanderer to break from the flow.

The heart seeks the mystery, the road less known,
To discover the seeds of the life we can own.
With each step we take, the old fades away,
Offering choices, come what may.

In unraveling threads of the paths that we roam,
We weave new connections, shaping our home.
Every twist, every turn, a chance to explore,
The beauty of living, forever, and more.

So set forth, dear dreamer, with courage in sight,
Embrace the unknown, let it guide you through night.
For on this grand journey, we'll rewrite our tale,
With each step we take, we will surely prevail.

The Road Less Travelled

In a world of paths well worn,
I pause beneath the trees,
Where whispers of the wild call,
And time dances with the breeze.

Each step feels light and free,
With dew upon the grass,
I venture down the unknown,
Curiosity unsurpassed.

The sun peeks through the leaves,
A golden touch of grace,
Leading me to hidden realms,
In this enchanted place.

No map to guide my way,
Just instinct as my light,
The road less travelled beckons,
With wonder burning bright.

Transcending Old Echoes

In the silence of the night,
Old echoes start to fade,
Memories like shadows linger,
Yet their grip is slowly laid.

Time unravels threads of pain,
Weaving hope into the light,
Letting go of past burdens,
Finding strength in the fight.

Each dawn brings a promise new,
A chance to rise and soar,
Transcending older whispers,
To embrace what lies in store.

With courage in my heart,
I step into the day,
Echoes turn to melodies,
In this vibrant ballet.

A Step into the Unknown

The edge of dusk invites me near,
A world that waits, unseen,
With questions on my lips, I tread,
Into the vast, serene.

The stars begin their dance above,
As shadows start to blend,
A symphony of hopes and dreams,
On this journey, I must depend.

I leave the comforts of the past,
With faith to guide my way,
A step into the unknown,
Where fears cannot sway.

In every breath I find my strength,
In every heartbeat, trust,
For the path ahead is uncharted,
But in it, I find thrust.

The Renaissance of Self

In whispers of the morning light,
I feel a spark ignite,
A canvas stretched before my eyes,
With colors shining bright.

With every brushstroke, I reclaim,
The pieces of my soul,
A renaissance unfolds within,
To finally become whole.

Through trials, I have grown anew,
Like flowers after rain,
Resilience blooms in vibrant hues,
Transforming all the pain.

Each day a new creation,
Each moment, pure and real,
In the art of becoming,
I discover what I feel.

Voices of Inner Clarity

In whispers soft, the truths arise,
Guiding hearts through shadowed skies.
A melody of thoughts, so pure,
Unlocking doors, where dreams endure.

With every breath, the silence speaks,
A journey found, the spirit seeks.
Through tangled doubts, a path is made,
Embracing light, the fears do fade.

Unveiling New Horizons

The dawn breaks forth, a canvas bright,
Colors blend in morning light.
With courage found, we reach afar,
Chasing dreams, our guiding star.

Through valleys low and mountains high,
New paths await beneath the sky.
With open hearts, we take the chance,
To dance with life, a wild romance.

Steps Over the Rubble of Regret

In rubble strewn, the past does lie,
Yet from the dust, we learn to fly.
Each step we take, a heart's refrain,
Forging strength from all the pain.

With every stride, we shed the weight,
Reclaiming joy, we change our fate.
From ashes rise, the spirit free,
Creating paths to who we'll be.

Beyond the Landscape of Comfort

In cozy nooks where dreams reside,
The call of change, we can't divide.
With open eyes, we seek the new,
Beyond the edge, where skies are blue.

Adventures wait in fields untamed,
Each heartbeat wild, unashamed.
To forge ahead, we must embrace,
The journey smiles, in every space.

The Light After the Storm

The clouds pull back, the sun peeks through,
A gentle warmth, a sky so blue.
Raindrops shimmer on the grass below,
Hope emerges in the afterglow.

Textures bright, the world seems new,
Life awakens, colors imbue.
A heart once heavy, now feels light,
We rise again, in the warm sunlight.

Strength is found in every tear,
The path ahead is now quite clear.
For in the darkness, we find our way,
A brighter dawn greets a brand-new day.

So let the thunder roll and roar,
For peace awaits on the shore.
Through trials faced, we learn to trust,
The light after the storm is a must.

Seeds of New Possibilities

In silence, we plant the seeds of fate,
With dreams as rich, we cultivate.
A whisper of hope in the morning air,
Each moment nurtured with tender care.

From tiny beginnings, greatness will grow,
Through shadows and storms, the roots will know.
The wind may whistle, the rain may fall,
Yet still they rise, breaking through it all.

Vision unfolds in the heart's embrace,
With courage, we stand, we find our place.
Every struggle a step on the climb,
To reach new heights and dance with time.

So plant your dreams, let them take flight,
With open hands, we invite the light.
For each seed sown blooms in its way,
New possibilities sprout day by day.

Embracing the Unfamiliar

In the shadows, new worlds await,
Beyond the horizon, we redefine fate.
With trembling hands, we reach for the sky,
In each brave step, we learn to fly.

The untraveled path, a whisper of chance,
In the unknown, let us dance.
With every heartbeat, a chance to learn,
In curiosity's fire, our spirits burn.

What if the risk leads to joy untold?
Or friendship forged, as hearts unfold?
Together we wander through lands unknown,
Building a future, forever our own.

So take my hand, let's leap into the new,
The sun will shine; our visions in view.
For life's great adventure, we hold the key,
In embracing the unfamiliar, we are free.

Awakening the Inner Phoenix

In the ashes of doubt, a fire ignites,
Resilience blooms in the darkest nights.
From dreams long buried, a spark emerges,
The phoenix rises, as the spirit urges.

With each new dawn, we shed our past,
Strength found in trials, a love to last.
Wings stretch wide through the thickened air,
With courage in hearts, we dare to care.

The flames of change flicker and sway,
Guide us forward on this bright new day.
Fear melts away with each brave flight,
We find our voice, embracing the light.

So rise, dear heart, let your colors shine,
For through the ashes, our souls align.
Awakening the fire, we ignite the spark,
To soar like a phoenix, bright in the dark.

Transforming Tides

The ocean whispers secrets true,
As waves crest high and fall anew.
Each rolling swell, a chance to grow,
Beneath the moon's soft, silver glow.

The shore shifts forms, a dance so grand,
With every touch of sea and sand.
A cycle known since time began,
Transforming tides, a master plan.

In moments still, the world finds peace,
As currents pull, and fears release.
The strength of water, fierce and kind,
Embraces souls that seek to find.

As dawn breaks bright, the tides will turn,
In every heart, a flame will burn.
With every wave, a story told,
Of changing paths, and dreams unfold.

A Journey to Reclaim

With weary feet, I trace the past,
A winding road, none traveled fast.
Each step, a memory to embrace,
A journey taken, seeking grace.

Through valleys low and mountains high,
I search for truths that never die.
With courage as my faithful guide,
I navigate the shifting tide.

The heart, a compass, points the way,
Through shadows dark and light of day.
With every loss, a chance to grow,
To find the strength in ebb and flow.

A moment's breath, the world stands still,
I gather courage, bend my will.
With hope restored, I rise anew,
A journey's end, a life in view.

Waking From the Gloom

In silence deep, the shadows creep,
Where dreams once soared, now secrets sleep.
Yet in the night, a spark will gleam,
Awakening the lost, a distant dream.

A whisper soft, a tender plea,
To break the chains that bind the free.
With every dawn, a chance to see,
The colors bloom, a tapestry.

From darkness thick, the light will spring,
And hope, like birds, will learn to sing.
Each moment born from sorrow's clutch,
Will turn to gold with gentle touch.

So rise, brave heart, embrace the sun,
For in this life, the battle's won.
Waking from the deepened gloom,
To fill the world with vibrant bloom.

The Art of Letting Go

In stillness found, a breath held tight,
We learn to dance with fading light.
Releasing dreams, we once held dear,
The art of letting go brings near.

With every thread that starts to fray,
We find the courage to drift away.
In gentle hands, the past must fade,
For new seeds sown, bring bliss displayed.

Each tear that falls, a river flows,
A testament to what we chose.
The heart will mend, with time bestowed,
In truth, we find the path we've strode.

So let the wind carry our fears,
Embrace the joy, release the tears.
For in this dance, we learn to grow,
The art of living is in letting go.